1

Windows, Absolute Basics for Beginners

by
Bill Rosoman Dip CS

Copyright 2014 Bill Rosoman Dip CS
All Rights Reserved,
No reproduction in any form without
the permission of the Author,

ISBN 978-1-927-157-44-2

Table of Contents

About the Author

I am currently publishing and writing Books and Ebooks. This is interesting and fun. I am also making some money!
https://www.smashwords.com/profile/view/leftfieldnz
http://goo.gl/UZscms

Many of my books on technology, Windows, Android and Linux.

My biggest sellers are on Desktop Publishing
https://www.smashwords.com/books/view/32052
https://www.smashwords.com/books/view/49688

I have worked with technology for many years and have been quite prophetic over the years. I have been working on Books and Ebooks online for many years now. It is starting to pay some dividends and we are starting to get some rewards.

I am also a Trademe Entrepreneur (it is like Ebay)
http://goo.gl/60wrLY

Selling small items for smartphones and tablets.

Our website is at www.creativekiwis.com

Disclaimer

The author, publisher and distributors of this book will in no manner whatsoever assume any responsibility, or liability of any kind for advice or methods provided in this book and used by the reader of this book. The reader assumes all responsibility and liability for his or her actions, as a result of reading this book and using ideas found herein.

In a number of places advice and/or recommendations are given regarding particular companies and their services, and I would like to state that I am in no way employed by any of the companies or services being recommended or suggested, or being paid any fees of any kind for mentioning these companies and their services.

No warranties or guarantees of any kind are being made or implied by the author or publisher as to the reliability or soundness of any of these companies or services being mentioned or recommended. No liability of any kind whatsoever is or will be assumed by the author or publisher.

All Copyrights and Trademarks are acknowledged.

Introduction

See it is REAL Easy!

The biggest thing about computers, is to give it a go and to try something new.

It is very hard to destroy a computer or the software that drives it during normal use, unless you throw it out the window.

As long as you follow a few simply rules and do a bit of house keeping on your Computer you should be fine.

If things go really wrong turn off the computer and go and have a coffee, it is probably something real simple that will fix the problem!

But above all have a bit of fun.

I use Computers to a lot of their potential and am self-taught, Press a few buttons and see what happens.

Push a button, give it a go or do a Google Search (Google is your friend).

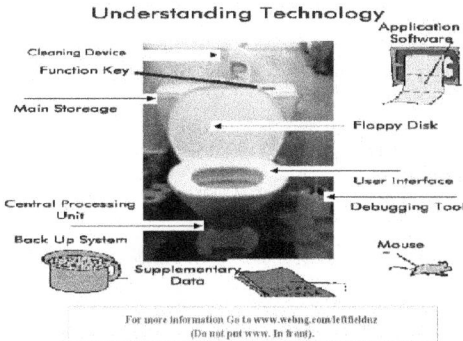

Understanding Technology

For more information Go to www.webng.com/leftfieldnz
(Do not put www. In front).

The Cardinal Rules of Using Computers and in particular Windows.

✓ *Save your work often and in a location and with a name you can remember easily.*
✓ *Do not use MS Internet Explorer, it is a shocking program, use Google Chrome or Mozilla Firefox instead.*
✓ *Do some Housekeeping on your computer often, IE weekly or fortnightly.*
✓ *Have a break and a walk around often.*
✓ *If you are getting frustrated, go have a coffee or come back tomorrow and if the going gets real tough do a Google*
✓ *Do Not Forget your Passwords!*
✓ *But always have fun and enjoy life!*
✓ *Remember what you called a file and were you put it!*

You may need to start with getting an email account at www.gmail.com so you can set your new device up.

Car Analogy

Using Technology is like driving a Car.

You go to the trouble of getting your drivers license, buying a car and learning how to drive it using all the gears etc.

You also know it needs some petrol, oil and water now and then.

So how come with computers some people will not even start the motor or they drive around the internet in 1st gear refusing to know or use the other gears let alone hit 100km (60mph) on the motorway!

So get the old computer out of the garage, get it started and zoom around the world online in 80 seconds LOL.

Setup Your Computer, Tablet

Most computers, tablets, smartphones come with the basics, but you need some more and better software.

See the next chapter for Basic Free Software.

Then look at the chapter on Housekeeping.

You will need access to the internet, via a Hotspot (using your smartphone), or Wireless Access (WIFI).

Wifi can be free at a Library or some places lie McDonalds, Some Motels/Hotels have free or pay access to WIFI.

Or you can have home broadband internet access with WIFI.

http://help.spark.co.nz/app/answers/detail/a_id/9885/~/all-about-wifi-at-home
http://www.pcadvisor.co.uk/how-to/mobile-phone/3441165/how-use-your-smartphone-as-wi-fi-hotspot/

Basic Free Software

The basic software you need is available online and free.

Most of the suggested software is multi-platform, Windows, Android, MacOS, Linux.

Install Google Chrome Web Browser
https://www.google.com/chrome/?

Download, Install then Login with your Gmail account to take full advantage of what Google has to offer and its all for free.

Download Software
Save to Downloads
Bottom Left Show Progress of Download
When Download Finished, Click on File to Install

Using Google Chrome
https://www.youtube.com/watch?v=GgCSVih3Ub4

Install Kingsoft Office now WPS Office (same as Microsoft Office)

Kingsoft is exactly the same as MS Office, but free.
http://www.kingsoftstore.com/kingsoft-office-freeware
http://www.wps.com/

Kingsoft Office Suite Free 2013 is perhaps the most versatile free office suite, which includes free word processor, spreadsheet program and presentation maker. These three programs help you deal with office tasks with ease:
 Writer - Efficient word processor;
 Presentation - Multimedia presentations creator;
 Spreadsheets - Powerful tool for data processing and data analysis

Although it is a free suite, Kingsoft Office comes with many innovative features, including a paragraph adjustment tool, and multiple tabbed feature. It also has Office to PDF converter, automatic spell checking and word count features.
 The latest free Office 2013 supports saving files as DOCX and XLSX. Learn more.

Download and Install.

Using an Office Suite of Programs

This is some information in how to create or edit a Document or a Spreadsheet or even a Presentation.

Especially nowadays we have many choices for when we want to write a letter or do a spreadsheet or even a presentation.

There is the traditional Microsoft Office (Word, Excel, Powerpoint).
MS Office is not free. Where as all the rest are.

But there is also Open Office, Libre Office, Kingsoft etc.
Most of the MS Office Alternatives are also Multi-Platform i.e. Windows, Mac, IOS (Apple), Android, Linux.

We can also use Cloud computing – (Online using a Webrowser) which simply means using the internet, rather than your own computers, to store files and software – offers an alternative. It can provide access from any device with an internet connection, including tablet computers and smartphones, although screen size may make access tricky with the latter. And you can get everything offered by Microsoft Office, along with some interesting extras, from Google for free at a basic level.

https://drive.google.com

Tutorials
http://seniornet-huntly.webnode.com/
http://www.gcflearnfree.org/
http://office.microsoft.com/en-us/training-FX101782702.aspx

Install Foxit PDF Reader
http://www.foxitsoftware.com/downloads/

Do not use Adobe PDF reader as it is Bloatware.

Download Software
Save to Downloads
Bottom Left Show Progress of Download
When Download Finished, Click on File to Install

Install Gimp Photo/Graphics Editor

http://www.gimp.org/downloads/
Excellent free program to editor and manipulate photos.
Download Software
Save to Downloads
Bottom Left Show Progress of Download
When Download Finished, Click on File to Install

Install VLC Multi-Media Player

http://www.videolan.org/vlc
This will play most multi-media types.
Download Software
Save to Downloads
Bottom Left Show Progress of Download
When Download Finished, Click on File to Install

Install Mozilla Firefox Web Browser

https://www.mozilla.org/en-US/firefox/fx/#desktop
Download Software
Save to Downloads
Bottom Left Show Progress of Download
When Download Finished, Click on File to Install

Install Mozilla Thunderbird Email Client

Download Software, google thunderbird

www.mozzila.org/thunderbird
Download Software
Save to Downloads
Bottom Left Show Progress of Download
When Download Finished, Click on File to Install
Read Onscreen Help if Needed
Click Run
Follow Install Instructions
Agree Yes to Run
Press Next
Press Standard and Next
Install
Launch Thunderbird, Click Finish
Add Account
Enter Email Address and Password
Click Next, and it should setup for you
Now Email should work
To get new mail click Get Mail
To write a new Email Click on Write

https://www.youtube.com/watch?v=-GdGctGhltU

Use Windows live Email Client

Download Software, google Windows Live email
www.windows.microsoft.com/en-nz/windows-live/essentials
Download Software
Save to Downloads
Bottom Left Show Progress of Download
When Download Finished, Click on File to Install
Agree Yes to run
What do you want to Install?
Choose Programs
Unclick all except Mail
Install
Program will be installed

When completed press Close
In Windows XP or 7 it is on the Menu (Start Menu)
On Windows 8 it is by pressing the Windows Button, type live, right click on the Icon and Pin to Taskbar
Run MS Live Email
Accept the terms
Enter Email Address and Password and Display Name
Click Next, Click Finish
Your Email will be downloaded

Pokki Email Client

This s neat little program especially for windows 7/8/8.1

http://www.pokki.com/download/?name=Gmail&etag=Pokki_Gmail

Use Mail App (windows 8+)

We are now tying to encourage our selves and others to use apps.
Windows 8 has an app for mail.

Use Pixlr Online Picture Editor

http://pixlr.com/
An excellent online picture editor

Use Zamzar Online File Converter

www.zamzar.com

Will convert any format to any format, say PDF to Doc, Jpg to Png enc.

Use Online Tutorials

http://seniornet-huntly.webnode.com/
http://www.gcflearnfree.org/
http://office.microsoft.com/en-us/training-FX101782702.aspx

Install Skype

www.skype.com

Skype is a good VOIP Internet Phone, Chat, Video program or app.

Or you can get an internet phone number at www.2talk.co.nz and use Zoiper to run on any device to have a global phone number.

https://www.youtube.com/watch?v=ctveC5q9i0E

More Free Software

http://seniornet-huntly.webnode.com/software/

Get a Gmail Account

https://www.gmail.com/intl/en/mail/help/about.html

By getting a gmail account Google supplies free, loads of apps and tools like,

Google Drive
Google Calendar
Google Contacts
Google Hangouts
Google Analytics
Google Addsense
Youtube
Google Search
Google Maps
Google Earth
Google Translate
Etc etc

More Google Stuff
http://seniornet-huntly.webnode.com/google/

So much fun and all payed for by adds.

I make money from a share of the adds on www.youtube and on our website www.creativekiwis.com

Basic Windows House Keeping

With Windows Operating System there is a need to protect the computer from Viruses, Spyware, Malware, Phishing, Cookies etc.

Windows 8+ comes with virus protection from windows, on older computers use www.avast.com or another free virus checker like http://www.clamav.net/index.html

As well as this there is a need to do some computer house keeping to make the computer run smoother and faster.

On the Desktop, in a spare place, Right Click, Select New and Create a Folder called Housekeep.

From the Desktop if you see a virus checker or a program like Spybot, Drag them an Drop them Into the Housekeep Folder.

Open the Housekeep Folder and Right Click, New, Shortcut, Type in cleanmgr, Next, Rename Clean Manager and OK.

This is to run clean manager once a week or fortnight to delete, old and obsolete files enc.

Now Right Click, New, Shortcut, Type in defrgui.exe for windows 7-8 or dfrg.msc for Windows XP, Next, Rename Defrag and OK.

Run this Monthly and see if the Computer needs Defrag.

In case you are wondering, Defrag Makes the Non-contiguous files contiguous, IE makes it easy for windows to find a file and run it faster.

Now for older computers install Spybot for spyware and malware.
Download Spybot
http://www.safer-networking.org/dl/
Just make sure you stick to the free version and not download a lot of rubbish. Install and run once a week or fortnight to clean

the computer.

For   new   computers   install
http://www.superantispyware.com/download.html
Superspyware.

For heavy duty cleaning of the computer use cc cleaner.
http://www.piriform.com/ccleaner/download
Make sure to download the free version.
Use CC Clean with a bit of caution as it does some major things, but will give the computer a good clean out.

https://www.youtube.com/watch?v=vbxPL8oIyOI

Windows Shutdown Shortcut

On a blank space on the Desktop, Right click, Create New, Shortcut
Enter, Shutdown.exe -s -t 00
Click, Next
Rename Shutdown and Click, Finish
Now Right Click on the Desktop Icon, Select Properties, Change Icon, OK, Select the Red Power Off Icon, Click OK twice.
Now Right click on the Bottom Toolbar and make sure it is Unlocked.
Drag the Icon and Drop into the Toolbar.
Now when you click on the Icon the Computer will shutdown immediately.
https://www.youtube.com/watch?v=AO0rQqlIAig

The Basics

You must carry out some basic maintenance on your computer or you will have problems.

Most computers nowadays come with an anti-virus program. However, many people fail to

keep their database of virus definitions updated. All the major anti-virus programs come with an update feature that should be used regularly. Having to update daily is now routine since new malware appears constantly.(Note that anti-virus programs actually protect against a variety of malware, not just viruses.)

You need to have a good Viruses Checker, a good Spyware Cleaner and a good Firewall to keep as many of the nasties from the Internet at bay.

Some Suggestions for Software

NB all the suggested software is free.

virus checker

windows security essentials (not for XP) http://www.microsoft.com/en-us/download/details.aspx?id=29942

Avast http://www.avast.com/index
If you need a virus checker.
.
For XP try http://www.clamwin.com/

Ccleaner to remove trash and old files
https://www.piriform.com/ccleaner/download

Adaware http://lavasoft.com

spyware spybot http://www.safer-networking.org/mirrors

NB Windows 8 has Windows Defender Installed by default, you do not need another virus checker.

Updating anti-spyware protection These days, anti-virus programs are insufficient to guard against all malware. Anti-spyware programs are also needed and like anti-virus programs must be updated regularly. Some programs are automatic some are not. If you do not see the Virus Checker and Spyware Cleaner Automatically Updating, right click on the program on the right hand side of the toolbar and update from there.

Preparing for disaster Unfortunately, hard drive failure is not all that uncommon. If it occurs, everything that is on the drive is lost (unless you resort to an expensive recovery service).

Also, if you do get a virus, a lot of your disk may be wiped out. Or, in a variety of other ways, files may be corrupted or lost. Botched software installations, system crashes, or just plain carelessness can lose valuable data. Thus, backups are essential. Ideally, the whole system should be backed up to some external storage device. At a minimum, all files such as passwords, favourite places, address books, financial and tax records, important documents and correspondence (including e-mail), and any other personal data that has more than transitory value should be backed up to some place other than your hard drive. Windows you can also share with family and friends. If you have a gmail account then you can use that by logging into Google Drive.

Using System Restore System Restore does not replace a regular backup procedure but the Windows XP/Vista/7/8 accessory. System Restore is a valuable tool that can remedy many common problems.

System Restore will restore your System to a previous date, but it wipes out all changes made after the Restore Date, so only should be used as a last resort, or if you have good back ups of all your important data.

Automatic Windows Updates

1. Click Start, and then click Control Panel. Depending on which Control Panel view you use, Classic or Category, do one of the following:
2. Click System, and then click the Automatic Updates tab.
3. Click Performance and Maintenance, click System, and then click the Automatic Updates tab.
4. Click the option that you want. Make sure Automatic Updates is not turned off.
5. If you do not have good access to the internet you may consider turning automatic updates and do them Manually when it is convenient.
6. With XP turn off the updates as it is no longer supported.

Internet Basics

The internet is amazing, forget watching TV, buying a paper, going to the shopping mall, going to the movies. Now it is all online and in most cases free.

A newspaper costs round about $300 per annum, SkyTV about $600 etc. You can get high speed unlimited broadband for $75 per month in NZ and other smaller packages around $50 per month, and watch all movies and read all the newspapers you wish for that one price!

You buy a lotto and check the results, do your banking online.

The internet is only limited by your imagination.
Get some information http://www.wikipedia.org/
Start a Blog www.wordpress.com
Get a weather forecast
http://www.accuweather.com/en/nz/hamilton/256405/weather-forecast/256405

Tutorials
http://www.gcflearnfree.org/internet
http://netforbeginners.about.com/od/internet101/u/inetbasics.htm

Basic Command Shortcuts

To make things a lot quicker using various Programs it is easy using a few of the Shortcut Keys and Just in Case You Forgot a few;

CTRL+C   Copy
CTRL+V   Paste
CTRL+X   Cut
CTRL+P   Print
CTRL+S   Save
CTRL+O   Open
CTRL+B   Bold
CTRL+U   Underline
CTRL+N   New File

CTRL+E   Center
CTRL+A   Se l e c t All
CTRL+R   Replace

F5   Reload/refresh or Go to a Page
F2   Rename
F3   Find   or CTRL+F

F7 Spell Check
HOME   Beginning of line
C T R L + HOME Beginning of file
END End of Line
CTRL + END End of File
DEL Delete
ALT+F4 Exit Program
ALT+F1 Menu
F 12 Bullets

Home Beginning of Row
End End of Row
Ctrl+Home Beginning of File
Ctrl+End End of File
Del Delete Highlighted
Insert Toggle between Insert and Over type
Page Up Up One Screen
Page Down Down One Screen
Caps Lock Capitals
Shift + Key Capital or alternative Key

These are the Basic Command Short Cuts and should work in most programs, of Cause you can go File > Save with you mouse but the Keyboard Short Cuts are so much easier and better on the hands.

Windows 8+ Basics

Windows 8 or 8.1 are a new way of doing things. From now on as is the case with Apple, Android etc. Everything will done using apps.

Apps are Applications what we used to call Programs

Now we use an app or even better use a Cloud App like Google Docs/Drive
https://drive.google.com

So we now encourage all people to Use Apps rather than Programs as this is the World we live in Now!

NB Please make sure the Windows 8 is up to date. There should be windows 8.1 and an update in mid-April 2014. To check go to, Control Panel, System and see what is installed.

To update go to the store and on the left it will show any updates needed.

Windows 8+ Apps

Apps are Applications what we used to call Programs.

Now we use an app or even better use a Cloud App like Google Docs/Drive.
https://drive.google.com

So we now encourage all people to Use Apps rather than Programs as this is the World we live in Now!

The only problem is some of the apps are not very mature and there are problems running them. Such is life!

Google Drive (Cloud Computing)

https://drive.google.com
https://www.youtube.com/watch?v=j0v9AVEGIjY
https://www.youtube.com/watch?v=Gw2CTN46tXg

Google Drive is for storing files up in the Cloud and for creating Documents, Spreadsheets, Presentations Online in the Cloud.

Your files are always waiting for you at http://drive.google.com , but you can also get them straight from your computer, Smartphone, and tablet. Install Google Drive on multiple devices and Google Drive makes sure they're all the same. You can even get to your files after you go offline.
Keep files synced. Just connect to the web – it's pretty much automatic.
Any time your device has Internet access, it checks in with Google Drive. That ensures your files and folders are always up to date. Change something on one device and it changes everywhere.
Stop emailing attachments. Start sharing.
Google Drive lets you choose exactly who – friends, family, colleagues – gets your files. You don't need email attachments any more. Just share your file, folder, or Google Doc from any

device.

Keep collaborating!

Do you collaborate with others in Google Docs, Sheets, and Slides? Google Drive lets you continue to create, access, and collaborate in a version-free world.

Google Drive also incorporates what used to be Google Docs. This means that you can create or edit a Word document, a Excel spreadsheet, powerpoint presentation, pixir graphic enc. without software on your computer and from anywhere in the world.

Google Calendar

https://www.google.com/calendar

Everyone has meetings to attend, parties with friends, or deadlines to meet. Scheduling these events using Google Calendar can keep you right on track. Let's say you have lunch with your friend every other Sunday and want to put the event on your calendar.

To create an event, select a date and a popup will appear asking for an event name, you can also edit the event from here.

Use Google Chrome Apps

https://chrome.google.com/webstore/category/apps

These are great to use as they are mostly online apps and you just need an internet connection and a Google Chrome Browser.

Google Syncing

One good thing using Google and Cloud Computing is that all your info is synced between the various device you have or have access to.

I use a smartphone, a tablet, a laptop and have access to other laptops etc.

If I save a document or a photo directly into the cloud then I know were it is and it is available on all my devices and I do not have to go looking for it.

It also means my stuff is safe in case I lose a device, a device gets stolen or a device dies.

It is also great if you are working as part of a team of people located in different places and countries.

Internet Banking

Have a look at this site;
https://sec.westpac.co.nz/IOLB/Login.jsp

For some more info
https://www.asb.co.nz/personal/banking-with-asb/internet-banking

Login

Westpac NZ
home page

Enter your Customer ID

Your security

Ask a question

Banking on your
mobile

Report a phishing
scam

Enter your password

1

Need help?

Reset your own password

2

Login

Westpac ONLINE BANKING GUARANTEE

Westpac ONLINE GUARDIAN

Norton
SECURED
powered by VeriSign

Internet banking is easy, safe and secure.

Internet banking can be done easily from a tablet or Smartphone using an App.

No more bank cues or paying a fee of $2.50 to pay your phone bill at the Post Shop!

Cloud Computing

This is to help you understand and use Cloud Computing.

Cloud Computing is the next big thing. It is about changing the way we think and do things.
We will only need a simple computer as long as it has access to the internet.
We will not need much software apart from a decent web browser and an email client.

Cloud computing is the use of computing resources (hardware

and software) that are delivered as a service over a network (typically the Internet). The name comes from the use of a cloud-shaped symbol as an abstraction for the complex infrastructure it contains in system diagrams. Cloud computing entrusts remote services with a user's data, software and computation.

Google Drive Cloud Storage, Create Online Documents, Spreadsheets and Presentations
https://drive.google.com

Tutorials
https://www.youtube.com/watch?v=Gw2CTN46tXg
https://www.youtube.com/watch?v=wpniwgtfxHU

Linux a Free Windows Alternative OS

I use Linux Mint 17. Apart from the L word it is much the same as Windows but it is all free and there are no Viruses, Spyware.

Linux Users similar programs like WPS Office, Google Chrome, Gimp, VLC Media Player etc.

You can even run some Windows Programs or install Windows via Virtualbox withing Linux, as I do.

So there are many options.

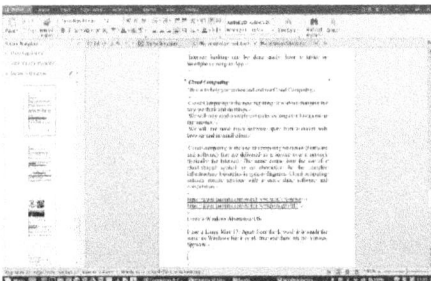

This is my Linux Desktop.
http://www.linuxmint.com/

There are many Flavours of Linux Mint is one of the most popular.

You can easily run Windows files like .doc or .docx.

Linux Mint 13 is a great replacement on older computers running the un-supported Windows XP (abandon ware).

I avoid Windows as much as I can.

A Preview of Linux Mint
https://www.youtube.com/watch?v=EeD9WQh3SbQ

Some Online Websites of Interest

Facebook

Facebook is a great place to keep in touch and chat to friends and family.
www.facebook.com

Youtube

www.youtube.com
You can download or watch Movies, Music, Documentaries, Cartoons etc.

Spotify

Spotify: Music for everyone
https://www.spotify.com
Spotify is a digital music service that gives you access to

millions of songs.

Ebay

Ebay is were you can buy and sell all sorts of stuff.

www.ebay.com

Trademe is the NZ equivalent www.trademe.co.nz

Online News
http://www.bbc.com/news/world/
http://edition.cnn.com/WORLD/

News from around the world.

Free Newspapers

http://www.huffingtonpost.com/
http://www.nzherald.co.nz/
http://www.nytimes.com/
http://www.telegraph.co.uk/

TV On Demand

http://tvnz.co.nz/video
http://www.tv3.co.nz/OnDemand.aspx
http://xfinitytv.comcast.net/ondemand/full_episodes#page=1&s
ortBy=fancastVodRank&layout=gallery
http://www.sbs.com.au/ondemand/

Free Online Games

http://www.freeonlinegames.com/
http://www.miniclip.com/games/en/

Free Sports Online

http://www.stream2u.me/
http://livetv.sx/en/
http://www.firstrowsports.bz/

Online Free Education

edX | Free online courses from the world's best universities
https://www.edx.org

EdX offers free online courses and classes. Find the latest MOOC from the world's best universities including MIT, Harvard, Berkeley, UT and others.

If you are Bored!

How to Waste Time Online - 33 Things to do when you are ...
www.blifaloo.com/boredom.php

Boredom relief with 33 fun and interesting ways to waste time on the internet.

Free Stuff - Games - Optical Illusions - Zombie Quiz!
Top 10 things to do on the Internet when you're bored
http://www.jogtheweb.com/flat/6Io6YRb2q2Hp/Top-10-things-to-do-on-the-Internet-when-youre-bored

a list of things to do when you are bored... ... 8. Search up random things on Youtube and see what comes up.

http://www.youtube.com . View this page. internet ...

Im so Bored - Bored Site - PointlessSites.com
www.pointlesssites.com/tools.asp
Tools and utilities for the things you didn't know you needed

tools and utilities for. ... Comment parrot - Do you rage online at people you don't know? Then you   ...
20 Fun Things To Do Online When You're Bored At Work
www.makeuseof.com/tag/20-fun-online-bored-work

Jan 5, 2012 - Office Workspace Cubicle 20 Fun Things To Do Online When Youre Bored At Work We all love working, don't we? I'm sure none of you reading

Online Gambling, dating, etc.

Tutorial
https://www.youtube.com/watch?v=qXLqDTMOY24

What Next!

The world of technology is moving at a staggering pace.

There is going to be a technology explosion with many things like books, music, shopping, banking etc moving online.

The next generation will be digital natives and will not know what a stamp or letter are, or a music or movie DVD.

Shopping Voting, Banking dealing with Government will all be online.

Moore's law - Wikipedia, the free encyclopedia
http://en.wikipedia.org/wiki/Moore's_law

In 1975 Moore slowed his forecast regarding the rate of density-doubling, stating circuit density-doubling would occur every 24 months. And it has and is.

I already have my NZ Government ID approved,

www.realme.govt.nz and do a lot of my Government stuff online.

http://en.wikipedia.org/wiki/Future_Technology

My Online World

My YouTube Chanel https://www.youtube.com/user/leftfieldnz
My website http://leftfieldnz.webnode.com/
My Blog http://leftfieldnz.wordpress.com/
My other Blog http://digitalcrusade.wordpress.com/
Facebook https://www.facebook.com/pages/Creative-Kiwis/131693886876416
Books and Ebooks site
www.creativekiwis.com

I have been online since the 1980s. We had Pacnet, Starnet then the Internet.

My Starnet email was rde002.

Creative Kiwis an Amazing Journey.

We have many Books and Ebooks Available for your enjoyment and enlightenment.

www.creativekiwis.com

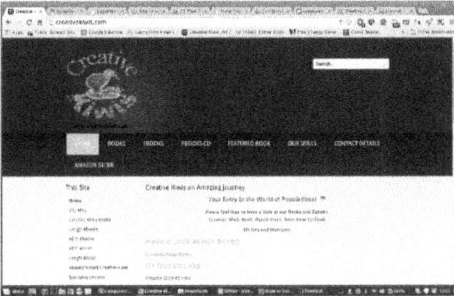

About Creative Kiwis

www.creativekiwis.com is a joint venture between Craig and Bill.

Creative Kiwis is our Empire, our Portal to the World.

It provides us with a Platform to Promote mostly our Books and Ebooks.

It has been a fantastic journey of discovery and enlightenment.

Bills Bio

Bill Rosoman's Dip CS Skills

Bill has;

a Diploma in Computing stream Support, Level five

30 years computer experience

a passion for computing, telecommunications and the internet

been an author and publisher for many years

been a successful Book/Ebook Publisher on

http://www.smashwords.com/profile/view/leftfieldnz

http://goo.gl/UZscms

http://goo.gl/WHbCde

been specialising in doing book layout, book covers and getting the books and ebooks published online and selling

If Bill can help you get your Book or Ebook Online or if you need a Website or similar contact him now

leftfieldnz@gmail.com

Craigs Bio

Craig Lock's BA Skills

Craig has;

a BA

Spent many years in the corporate world in South Africa and New Zealand. Financial Services.

written some brochures on Money Management

been an author and publisher for many years

been a successful Book/Ebook Publisher on

Amazon http://goo.gl/8Xawh

http://www.smashwords.com/profile/view/craiglock

Amazon **http://goo.gl/WvJOQH**

many years experience with internet promotion and marketing

many years experience in proof reading books

If Craig can help get your project off the ground contact him now

craiglock@xtra.co.nz

Creative Kiwis, an Amazing Journey.

Books, Ebooks, Audio Books and much more

www.creativekiwis.com

Bill Rosoman ebooks on Smashwords

http://www.smashwords.com/profile/view/leftfieldnz

Bill Rosoman Amazon.com books/ebooks

http://goo.gl/MLSLL

Craig Lock Amazon.com books/ebooks
http://goo.gl/vTpjk

Craig Lock ebooks on Smashwords
https://www.smashwords.com/profile/view/craiglock

Creative Kiwis Videos at
www.youtube.com/leftfieldnz

Creative Kiwis Blog

http://leftfieldnz.wordpress.com/

by   Bill Rosoman Dip CS

#####

www.ingramcontent.com/pod-product-compliance
Lightning Source LLC
Chambersburg PA
CBHW071801020426
42331CB00008B/2362